Twenty Poems

JOHN
HAINES

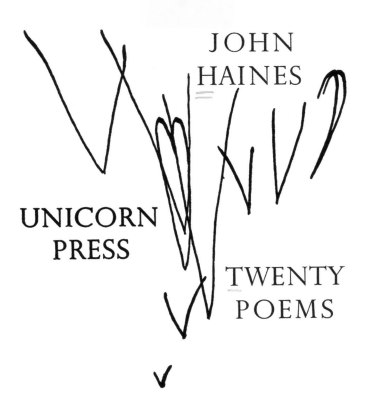

UNICORN
PRESS

TWENTY
POEMS

6/1972
am. Lit.

The poet and publisher want to thank the editors of the following magazines in whose pages most of these poems had previous appearances: *Chelsea; Chicago Review; Hudson Review; The Stand; Tampa Poetry Review : Tennessee Poetry Journal; Unicorn Folio* and *Unicorn Journal.*

The National Endowment for the Arts assisted the press at the time this book was being published.

Unicorn Press
P. O. Box 1469
Santa Barbara, California

To Jane
one night in Tehachapi

Twenty Poems

I

The Pitcher of Milk

Today is the peace of this mist
and its animals, as if all
the cows and goats in the land
gave milk to the dawn.

The same mist that rises
from battlefields, out of the mouths
and eye-sockets of horse
and man, it mingles with smoke
from moss fires
in the homesteader's clearing.

I and the others come to the doors
of cold houses, called
by the thin ringing of a spoon;

we stand with our brimming bowls,
called to where Peace awakens
in a cloud of white blood.

A Winter Light

We still go about our lives
in shadow, pouring the white cup full
with a hand half in darkness.

Paring potatoes, our heads
bent over a dream—
glazed windows through which
the long, yellow sundown looks.

By candle or firelight
your face still holds
a mystery that once
filled caves with the color
of unforgettable beasts.

The Invaders

It was the country I loved,
and they came over the hills
at daybreak.
        Their armor
hoisted a dirty flag to the dawn,
the cold air
glittered with harsh commands.

Up and down the roads of Alaska,
the clanging bootsoles,
the steely clatter of wheels,

treading down forests, bruising
the snows—
        bringing
the blossom of an angry sundown,

their cannon and blue flares
pumping fear into the night.

The Man Who Skins Animals

I

He comes down from the hill
just at dusk, with a faint
clinking of chains.

He speaks to no one, and when
he sits down by the fire
his eyes, staring into the
shadows, have a light like drops
of blood in the snow.

II

There is a small, soft thing
in the snow, and its ears
are beginning to freeze.

Its eyes are bright, but
what they see is not this world
but some other place
where the wind, warm and
well fed, sleeps
on a deep, calm water.

Woman

No one knows that country
who has not camped
at the foot of night's glacier.

Only he who has kindled his fire
in a wilderness of frozen men;

he alone has climbed the
sleeping breath of her mountain,
and at the summit
rested between the moon
and the morning star.

The Hermitage

In the forest below the stairs
I have a secret home,
my name is carved in the roots.

I own a crevice stuffed with moss
and a couch of lemming fur;
I sit and listen to the music
of water dripping on a distant stone,
or I sing to myself
of stealth and loneliness.

No one comes to see me,
but I hear outside
the scratching of claws,
the warm, inquisitive breath . . .

And once in a strange silence
I felt quite close
the beating of a human heart.

The Goshawk

I will not walk on that road again,
it is like a story one hesitates to begin.

You find yourself alone,
the fur close about your face, your feet
soft and quiet in the frost.

Then, with a cold, rushing sound,
there's a shadow like the death-angel
with buffeting wings,
his talons gripping your shoulder,
the bright beak tearing and sinking . . .

Then, you are falling, swept
into the deepening red sack of a voice:

"Little rabbit, you are bleeding again;
with his old fire-born passion
the Goshawk feeds on your timid heart."

Images of the Frost King

Once he stood at the door
like a birch unraveling in the wind.

He pounded the ice in his chest.
and his eyes were cold with grandeur.

In a mirror held by the forest
a cloud of aspens
leans upon a deserted throne.

The Frost King is sleeping,
his face darkened
by the flight of nocturnal thrushes.

II

The Sudden Spring

The coyote had just spoken
and lay down to rest in a snowdrift.

March, like a fly awakened too early,
droned between somnolence
and a furious boredom.

No one remembered the autumnal
prophet, teller of drowsy stories
to be continued . . .

Winter, the unfinished, the abandoned,
slumped like a mourner
between two weeping candles.

Larkspur

The blue giant is passing,
king of this field.

His trumpets blow pure cobalt,
he brings with him
audiences of the deepest indigo.

By his command
the sky-stained meadows overflow,
and bridges of azure
stretch far into evening . . .

where the king, his train halted,
stands alone in his blueness.

April

It was nothing but morning,
a bundle of plumes and a mountainpeak.

Beneath its mantle of wounds, the ice
delivered itself to a world of candles.

The mosquito's belly glowed,
and a strong black water burst from the ground,
like the burnt blood
from an old coffin of the sun.

Stones

They are dreaming existence.
One is a man, and one
is a woman. Beside them an animal,

someone who followed them
into the distance
until their feet grew heavy
and sank in the soil.

And the life within them became
an expanding shadow,
a blue gravel on which they fed
as they changed;

standing there so solid and dark,
as if they were waiting
for God to imagine their names.

The Mushroom Grove

Here the forest people
died of a sexual longing.

The ground trampled in their passion
healed into a cemetery,
with a few flowers
like frayed parachutes.

Their headstones are umbrellas,
black and weeping.

The Insects

Maggots, wrinkled white men
building a temple of slime.

Green blaze of the blowfly
that lights the labor of corpses.

The carrion beetle awakening
in a tunnel of drying flesh
like a miner surprised by the sun.

And rolling his bronze image
into the summer, the scarab,
whose armor shone once
in a darkness called Egypt.

III

The Dance

for George Hitchcock

The red armchair is empty.
The man who sat there
is turning in the room,
holding in his hands
a painted jungle.

The faces of his audience,
at first like flowers,
pale from lack of sunlight,
begin to darken
and put on the look
of watchers in a clearing.

No sound but a stealthy
scratching, and the slow steps
turning against smoke
and silence, as the dance
gathers everything
into a haunted forest . . .

From the bark of those trees
sprout flowers
like drops of blood,
and birds' heads
of a threatening blue.

Ryder

The moonlight has touched them all . . .

The dream hulk with its hollows
driven black,
the ancient helmsman, his handbones
glinting with salt and memory.

Under the sail of sleep, torn and flapping,
night's crowded whale broaches,
heaving another Jonah
to the shoal of a broken world.

Jehovah's arm outstretched
like a locust cloud at sea,

and the moon itself,
a pale horse of torment flying . . .

Paul Klee

The hot mice feeding in red,
the angry child
clutching a blue watermelon—
these are the sun and moon.

The Tunisian patch,
where beneath some crooked
black sticks
a woman's face is burning.

There are also disasters at sea,
compasses gone wrong—

only because of a gentle
submarine laughter,
no one is drowning.

Sleep

Whether we fall asleep under the moon
like gypsies, with silver coins
in our pockets, or crawl deep
into a cave through which the warm,
furry bats go grinning and flying,
or put on a great black coat
and simply ride away into the darkness,

we become at last like trees
who stand within themselves, thinking.

And when we awake— if we do—
we come back bringing the images
of a lonely childhood: the hands
we held, the threads we unwound
from the shadows beneath us;
and sounds as of voices in another room
where some part of our life
was being prepared—near which we lay,
waiting for our life to begin.

Spilled Milk

When I see milk spilled on the table,
another glass overturned,
I think of all the cows who labor in vain.

So many tons of forage spent,
so many udders filling and emptying,
forest after forest
stripped for paper cartons,
the wax from millions of candles melting . . .

A broad sheet of milk spills across
the tables of the world,
and this child stands
with a sopping sponge in his hand,
saying he never meant to do it.

Love Among The Oranges

There we stood howling
at the edge of town.
The small farms were sleeping,
mice and frogs in the grass.

In the big house
by the orange grove,
fire and drunkenness,
fierce, monotonous music.

But we were not going to go in;
there was something else
in the night, in the wind
that ruffled our fur,

in the shape of oranges
swaying in the moonlight,
falling around us
with a big, plump sound.

ϕ

485

COPIES OF THIS BOOK HAVE BEEN PRINTED
AT UNICORN PRESS: HAND-SET BY ALAN D.
BRILLIANT IN 14 PT PERPETUA; HAND-PRINTED
BY RUDY VILLANUEVA; HAND-BOUND BY
PATRICIA FIELD; ASSISTANCE BY ERIC SMITH,
TEO SAVORY, DANCI MOCK. THIS IS NUMBER

444